SIMPLIFIED SCAFFOLD EN
CONSTRUCTI...

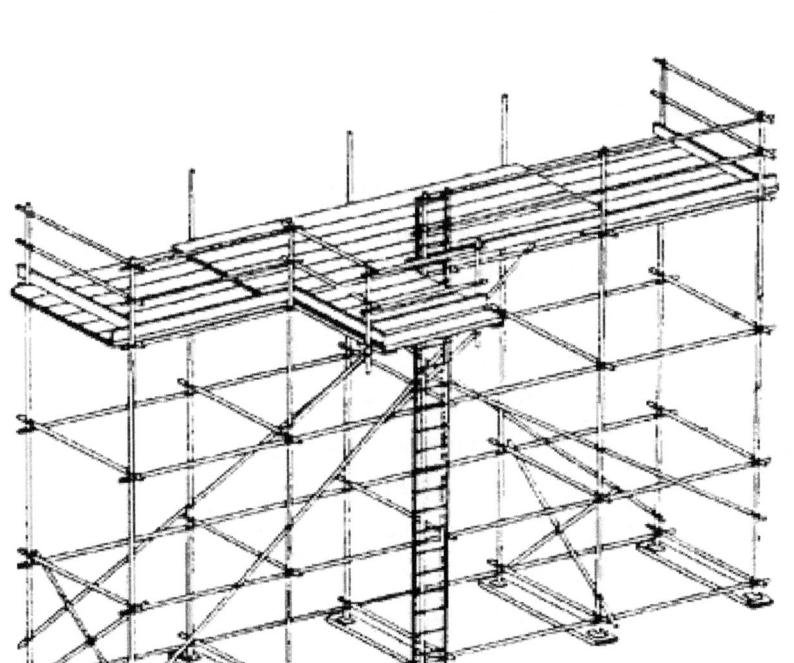

TABLE OF CONTENTS

	Page
1. Preface	5
2. Objectives	7
3. What is Scaffold	8
3.1 Tubes	9
3.2 Boards	9
3.3 Couplers	10
4. Types of Scaffold	11
4.1 Stationary Scaffold	11
4.2 Mobile Scaffold	12
4.3 Mobile/ Stationary Tower	12
4.4 Independent Scaffold	13
4.5 Indoor Mobile Scaffold	13
5. Scaffold Couplers	14
5.1 Types of Couplers	14
5.1.1 Base Plate	15
5.1.2 Right angle coupler	15
5.1.3 Putlog coupler	16
5.1.4 Swivel coupler	16
5.1.5 Spigot coupler	17
5.1.6 Sleeve coupler	18
5.1.7 Girder coupler	18
5.1.8 Wheels (caster)	19
6. Scaffold foundations	20
7. Standards	22
8. Ledger	23
9. Transforms	24
10. Brace	26

11.	Work platform		27
	11.1 Board lift		27
	11.2 Guardrails		28
	11.3 Handrail & Mid rail		29
	11.4 Toe board		29
	11.5 Ladder access		30
	11.6 Placing ladder		31
12.	Ladder Inspection		32
	12.1 Access		32
13.	System Scaffold		33
14.	Hazards In Construction and Use of Scaffold		36
	14.1 Falls		36
	14.2 Scaffold collapse		37
	14.3 Struck by falling materials		37
	14.4 Electrocution		38
	14.5 Summary on fall protection		39
15.	Fall protection while building or using scaffold		40
	15.1 Fall elimination		40
	15.2 Fall Prevention		41
	15.3 Fall Arrest		42
	15.4 Administrative Controls		43
16.	Scaffold Inspection		44
	16.1 When should you inspect Scaffold		44
	16.2 Who should inspect Scaffold		44
	16.3 How to inspect scaffold		44
	16.4 Scaffold base and structure		45
	16.5 Planks		46
17.	Scaffold tagging and Inspection		49
18.	Scaffold checklist		52
19.	Inspection report		54
20.	Scaffold hand over certificate		55

21. Common mistake Made with scaffolding	56
22. Common faults in scaffold structures	58
23. Conclusion	62

CHAPTER ONE
PREFACE

Scaffolding, also called scaffold or staging, is a **temporary structure** used to support a work crew and materials to aid in the construction, maintenance **and repair of buildings**, bridges and all other man-made structures. Scaffolds are widely used on site to get access to heights and areas that would be otherwise hard to get to.

Unsafe scaffolding has the potential to result in death or serious injury. Scaffolding is also used in adapted forms for formwork and shoring, grandstand seating, concert stages, access/viewing towers, exhibition stands, ski ramps, half pipes and art projects.

There are five main types of scaffolding used worldwide today. These are **Tube and Coupler** (fitting) components, prefabricated modular system scaffold components, H-frame / facade modular system scaffolds, timber scaffolds and bamboo scaffolds (particularly in China). Each type is made from several components which often include:

- A base jack or plate which is a load-bearing base for the scaffold.
- The standard, the upright component with connector joins.
- The ledger, a horizontal brace.
- The transom, a horizontal cross-section load-bearing component which holds the batten, board, or decking unit.
- Brace diagonal and/or cross section bracing component.
- Batten or board decking component used to make the working platform.
- Coupler, a fitting used to join components together.

- Scaffold tie, used to tie in the scaffold to structures.
- Brackets, used to extend the width of working platforms.

Specialized components used to aid in their use as a temporary structure often include heavy duty load bearing transoms, ladders or stairway units for the ingress and egress of the scaffold, beams ladder/unit types used to span obstacles and rubbish chutes used to remove unwanted materials from the scaffold or construction project.

The OSHA Standard, 29 CFR 1926.451, specifies performance requirements and methods of structural and general design for access and working scaffolds. Requirements given are for scaffold structures that rely on the adjacent structures for stability. In general these requirements also apply to other types of working scaffolds.

The purpose of a working scaffold is to provide a safe working platform and access suitable for work crews to carry out their work. The European Standard sets out performance requirements for working scaffolds. These are substantially independent of the materials of which the scaffold is made. The standard is intended to be used as the basis for enquiry and design

CHAPTER TWO
OBJECTIVES

- To give a better awareness and understanding of the regulations concerning;
    - The suitability of materials used to construction scaffolds.
    - The manner in which these materials should be erected to form the more common types of scaffolds.
    - The correct construction of boarded out platforms, handrails and ladder access common to all scaffolds.

CHAPTER THREE
WHAT IS A SCAFFOLD?

A scaffold is a temporary structure which provides access from which persons may work. It can also be used to support materials or equipment. Furthermore, scaffold is a safe working platform.

The spacing of the basic elements in the scaffold are fairly standard. For a general purpose scaffold the maximum bay length is 2.1 m, for heavier work the bay size is reduced to 2 or even 1.8 m while for inspection a bay width of up to 2.7 m is allowed.

The scaffolding width is determined by the width of the boards, the minimum width allowed is 600 mm but a more typical four-board scaffold would be 870 mm wide from standard to standard. More heavy-duty scaffolding can require 5, 6 or even up to 8 board's width. Often an *inside board* is added to reduce the gap between the inner standard and the structure.

The lift height, the spacing between ledgers, is 2 m, although the base lift can be up to 2.7 m. The diagram above also shows a kicker lift, which is just 150 mm or so above the ground.

Transom spacing is determined by the thickness of the boards supported, 38 mm boards require a transom spacing of no more than 1.2 m while a 50 mm board can stand a transom spacing of 2.6 m and 63 mm boards can have a maximum span of 3.25 m. The minimum overhang for all boards is 50 mm and the maximum overhang is no more than 4x the thickness of the board.

The basic components of scaffolding are tubes, couplers and boards.

3.1 Tubes

The basic lightweight tube scaffolding that became the standard and revolutionised scaffolding, becoming the baseline for decades, was invented and marketed in the mid-1950s. With one basic 24 pound unit a scaffold of various sizes and heights could be assembled easily by a couple of labourers without the nuts or bolts previously needed.

Tubes are usually made either of steel or aluminium; although there is composite scaffolding which uses filament-wound tubes of glass fibre in a nylon or polyester matrix, because of the high cost of composite tube, it is usually only used when there is a risk from overhead electric cables that cannot be isolated. If steel, they are either 'black' or galvanised. The tubes come in a variety of lengths and a standard diameter of 48.3 mm. (1.5 NPS pipe). The chief difference between the two types of metal tubes is the lower weight of aluminium tubes (1.7 kg/m as opposed to 4.4 kg/m). However they are more flexible and have a lower resistance to stress. Tubes are generally bought in 6.3 m lengths and can then be cut down to certain typical sizes. Most large companies will brand their tubes with their name and address in order to deter theft.

3.2 Boards

Boards provide a working surface for scaffold users. They are seasoned wood and come in three thicknesses (38 mm (usual), 50 mm and 63 mm) are a standard width (225 mm) and are a maximum of 3.9 m long. The board ends are protected either by metal plates called hoop irons or sometimes nail plates, which often have the company name stamped into them. Timber scaffold boards in the UK should comply with the requirements of BS 2482. As well as timber, steel or aluminium decking is used, as well as laminate boards. In addition to the boards for the working platform, there are sole boards which are placed beneath the scaffolding if the surface is soft or otherwise suspect, although ordinary boards can also be used. Another solution, called a scaffpad, is made from a rubber base with a base plate moulded inside; these are desirable for use on uneven ground since they adapt, whereas sole boards may split and have to be replaced.

3.3 Couplers

Couplers are the fittings which hold the tubes together. The most common are called scaffold couplers, and there are three basic types: right-angle couplers, putlog couplers and swivel couplers. To join tubes end-to-end joint pins (also called spigots) or sleeve couplers are used. Only right angle couplers and swivel couplers can be used to fix tube in a 'load-bearing connection'. Single couplers are not load-bearing couplers and have no design capacity.

Other common scaffolding components include base plates, ladders, ropes, anchor ties, reveal ties, gin wheels, sheeting, etc. Most companies will adopt a specific colour to paint the scaffolding with, in order that quick visual identification can be made in case of theft. All components that are made from metal can be painted but items that are wooden should never be painted as this could hide defects. Despite the metric measurements given, many scaffolders measure tubes and boards in imperial units, with tubes from 21 feet down and boards from 13 feet down.

CHAPTER FOUR
TYPES OF SCAFFOLD
4.1 Stationary Scaffold

- Scaffolding consisting of two rows or more of standards connected together longitudinally with ledgers and braces and transversely with transoms or putlogs.
- Stationary scaffolds can be built-up as high as the job requirements dictate. The vertical members must be kept plumb and straight to avoid eccentric loading and possible collapse. Rigid bracing, usually a combination of horizontal and diagonal bracing, is required to prevent swaying and displacement. The footing or anchorage for scaffolds must be sound, rigid, and capable of carrying the maximum intended load without settlement or displacement.

4.2 Mobile Scaffold

- A mobile scaffold usually has four standards one at each corner.
- These can be placed on the ground and wheels (caster) are used, so that the scaffold can be moved.
- Mobile scaffolds are similar to Stationary scaffolds except that they are wheel mounted. The maximum height of a mobile scaffold must not exceed four times the smallest dimension of its base.

4.3 Mobile/Stationary Towers

Indoor

- Stationary Tower - 4.0 times the SBD (Smallest Base Dimension)
- Mobile Tower - 3.5 times the SBD

Outdoor

- Stationary Tower - 3.5 times the SBD
- Mobile Tower - 3.0 times the SBD

4.4 Independent Scaffold

4.5 Indoor Mobile Scaffold

This Mobile system scaffold was erected and needing rakes to add stability

CHAPTER FIVE
SCAFFOLD COUPLERS

- Sometimes called scaffold fittings.
- These have been designed and tested to BS. 5973 (British Standards) Specifications.
- Because some of them is load bearing components, most fittings achieve a SWL (Safe Working Load).

5.1 Types of Couplers

- Base Plate
- Right Angle Coupler
- Putlog Coupler
- Swivel Coupler
- Spigot Coupler
- Sleeve Coupler
- Girder Coupler
- Wheels (casters)

5.1.1 Base Plate

- This is a metal plate with a peg in the middle used under the standards.
- Used for distributing and spreading the load from the standard to the scaffolds foundation.
- In some cases, a screw jack is attached to maintain the levelling of the platform if is erected in unlevelled ground

5.1.2 Right Angle Coupler

- Right angle coupler are also known as a Double Coupler.

- Used to connect ledgers to the standards.

- They have been designed and tested to achieve a right angle connection with a maximum safe working load of 630KG

5.1.3 Putlog Coupler

- Also called Clips and single clamp.
- Used to connect the transoms to the ledgers
- These fittings are only suitable for light duty use only.
- This putlog coupler is not a load bearing fitting.

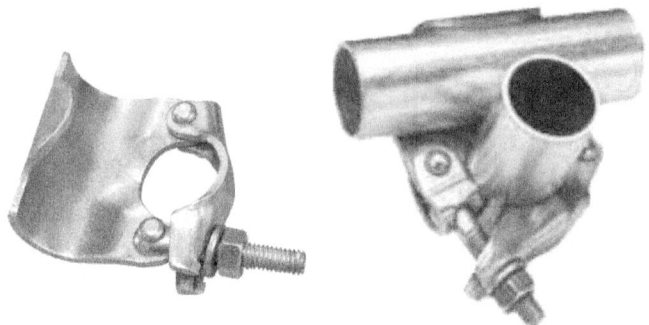

5.1.4 Swivel Coupler.

- Swivel couplers are used to connect two tubes at any angle through 360 degrees.
- Normally use to connect the bracing to the scaffold.

- The swivel coupler should never be used as a right angle coupler.

- This fitting is a load bearing coupler with an SWL of 550kg.

5.1.5 Spigot Coupler

- Also known as a joint pin.

- This fitting is used to connect two tubes together in longitudinal (end to end) and in vertical position.

- This fitting is placed inside the two ends of the tubes.

- This fitting should never be used in positions where it will be subject to bending or tension.

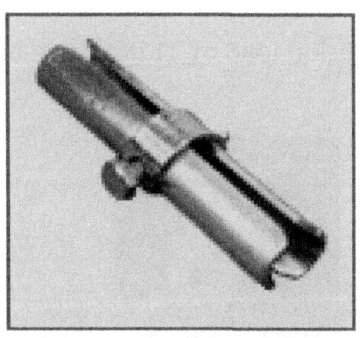 

5.1.6 Sleeve Coupler

- The sleeve coupler is used in the same way as the spigot coupler, but this time used on the outside of the tube.
- This fitting has a resistance to bending, at least equal to any tube.
- It has a safe working tension load of 315Kg.

5.1.7 Girder Coupler

- Girder Coupler or commonly known as Beam clamp. This coupler is used to connect the scaffolding pipe in to the beam.
- This fitting should always use in pairs to prevent movement.
- It has a safe working tension load of 315Kg if use in pairs.

5.1.8 Wheels (Caster)

- Wheels (casters) are used on towers allowing them to be moved.

- Wheels (casters) have two (2) locking systems.

- One to connect the wheel to the standard.

- One to lock the wheel in place to stop it moving.

CHAPTER SIX
SCAFFOLD FOUNDATIONS

Good scaffold foundations are essential. Often scaffold frameworks will require more than simple base plates to safely carry and spread the load. Scaffolding can be used without base plates on concrete or similar hard surfaces, although base plates are always recommended. For surfaces like pavements or tarmac base plates are necessary. For softer or more doubtful surfaces sole boards must be used, beneath a single standard a sole board should be at least 1,000 square centimetres (160 in^2) with no dimension less than 220 millimetres (8.7 in), the thickness must be at least 35 millimetres (1.4 in). For heavier duty scaffold much more substantial baulks set in concrete can be required. On uneven ground steps must be cut for the base plates, a minimum step size of around 450 millimetres (18 in) is recommended. A working platform requires certain other elements to be safe. They must be close-boarded, have double guard rails and toe and stop boards. Safe and secure access must also be provided.

The soil or ground beneath the sole board should be well compacted and free from irregularities, which could make the sole board unstable or poorly bedded.

On slopes exceeding 1:10 a check may have to be made on the foundations to ensure the stability of the scaffold. The ground must be capable of supporting the scaffold.

The sole boards must be capable of spreading the weight of the structure without distortion. Two standards per sole board are better than one.

Sole boards should be placed at right angles to the building and should not project too far out beyond the scaffold. Sole boards should not be undermined.

This diagram shows how the scaffold foundations should be corrected. Note that the cross braces have been added to transfer loading away from the base of those standards, which are near the trench

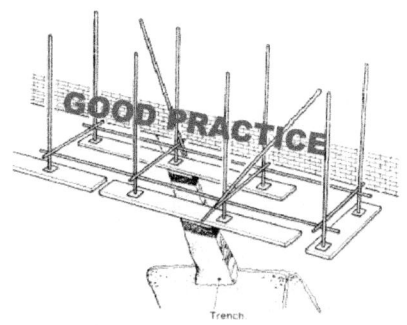

CHAPTER SEVEN
STANDARD

The standards, also called uprights, are the vertical tubes that transfer the entire weight of the structure to the ground where they rest on a square *base plate* to spread the load. The base plate has a shank in its centre to hold the tube and is sometimes pinned to a *sole board*. Ledgers are horizontal tubes which connect between the standards.

Scaffold use	Standard spacing{BS spacing (meters)}
Very light Duty Scaffold	2.7
Light Duty Scaffold	2.4
General Purpose Scaffold	2.1
Heavy Duty Scaffold	2.0

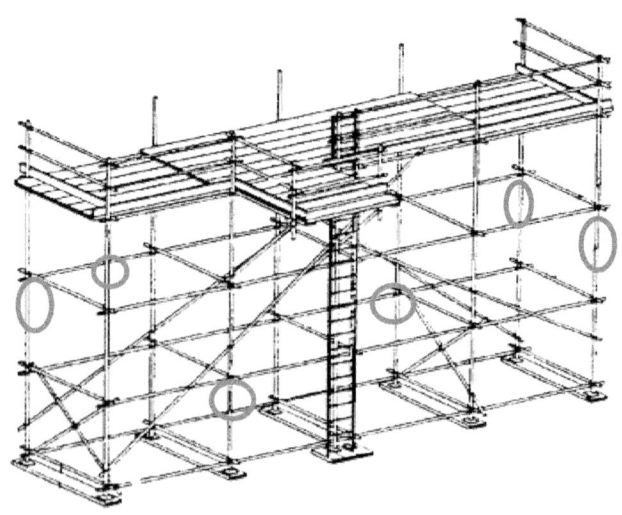

CHAPTER EIGHT
LEDGER

- A longitudinal tube fixed parallel to the face of the building.

- It also act as a support for the transoms.

- It can also be used to form part of the ties in the scaffold.

CHAPTER NINE
TRANSOMS

Transoms rest upon the ledgers at right angles. Main transoms are placed next to the standards, they hold the standards in place and provide support for boards; intermediate transoms are those placed between the main transoms to provide extra support for boards. In Canada this style is referred to as "English". "American" has the transoms attached to the standards and is used less but has certain advantages in some situations.

As well as the tubes at right angles there are cross braces to increase rigidity, these are placed diagonally from ledger to ledger, next to the standards to which they are fitted. If the braces are fitted to the ledgers they are called ledger braces. To limit sway a facade brace is fitted to the face of the scaffold every 30 metres or so at an angle of 35°-55° running right from the base to the top of the scaffold and fixed at every level.

- A tube spanning across the two ledgers to form support for the boards. It is sometimes called as the board bearers

- Maximum spacing between each transom is 1.5 metres. When a

38mm board is used.

- A minimum of four transoms to a 3.9 meter board.

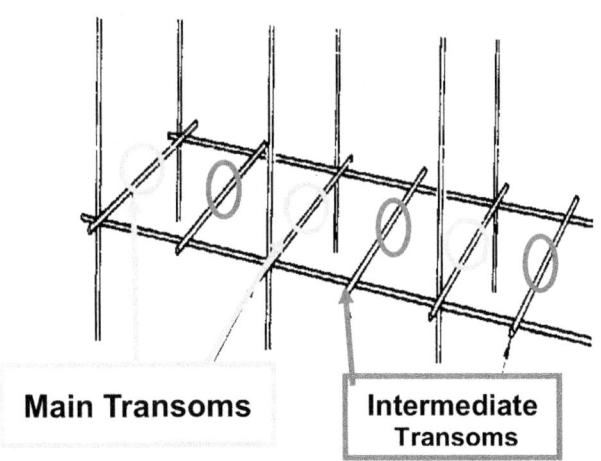

Main Transoms **Intermediate Transoms**

CHAPTER TEN
BRACE

- A tube placed diagonally with respect to the vertical or the horizontal members of a scaffold and fixed to them to afford stability.

- The best angle for setting the brace is 45 degrees.

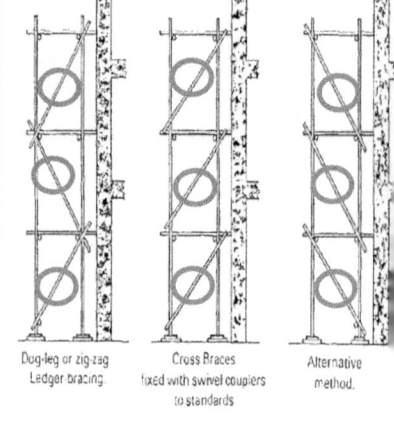

Dog-leg or zig-zag Ledger bracing.   Cross Braces fixed with swivel couplers to standards   Alternative method.

CHAPTER ELEVEN
WORK PLATFORM

All scaffold boards should comply with BS 2482; and should not be warped, twisted, split or badly worn, painted or otherwise treated so as to conceal any defects.

- <u>Two Boards wide</u>
    - Access Only
- <u>Three Boards wide</u>
    - For men without tools
- <u>Four Boards wide</u>
    - For men with tools

11.1 Boarded Lifts

- The spacing of transoms for the boarded lifts is limited by the thickness of boards used.

- While boards are available which are manufactured to BS 2482, the majority boards used on scaffolding will conform to NASC Technical guidance Note TG5:91 (Scaffold Board Specification).

- 38mm boards made to TG5:91 standard should be supported at a maximum span of 1.2 meters whereas, when a BS board is employed, a maximum span of 1.5 meters may be used.

Maximum spacing for putlogs or transoms when using boards conforming to BS 2482

Nominal Thickness of board	Maximum span of transom
32mm	1.0 meter
38mm	1.5 meter
50mm	2.6 meter
63mm	3.5 meter

11.2 Guard-rails

- Guard-rails must be provided:
- Where persons are liable to fall 2 meters or more
- At a level at least 910mm above the level of the platform
- At the height approximately halfway between the top edge of the toe-board and the top or subsequent guard-rail, so that no gap is larger than 470mm
- And fixed inside the standards

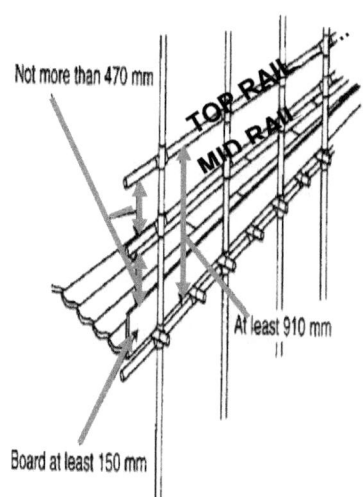

11.3 Handrails, Mid-rails

11.4 Toe boards

| Toe-boards must be provided:
 • Toe boards must be fitted to all scaffolds to prevent persons and materials falling from the scaffold. It must be installed in all sides of the scaffold platform except in access point.
 • To accompany guard-rails.
 • At least 150mm high above the platform (they are usually made by scaffold board turned on edge) | 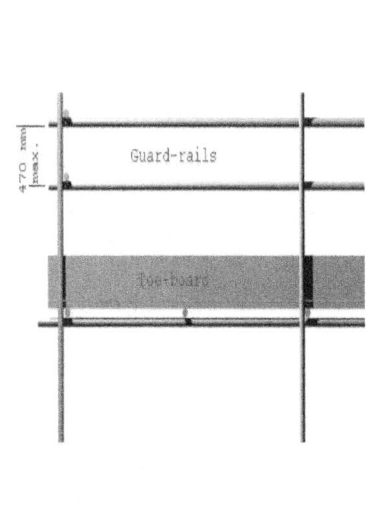 |

| - And fixed inside the standard with the use of proper clips | |

11.5 Ladder access

Ladders used as access to the workplace should be:

- Not defective in any way nor painted
- Placed on a firm footing, with each stile equally supported
- So positioned that there is sufficient space at each rung to give an adequate foothold
- Positioned approximately at an angle of 75º, that is: 1 measure horizontal to 4 measures vertical
- When more than 3 meters in length it must be securely tied at the top or footed at the bottom to prevent slipping
- Extended to a height of 1 meter (5 rungs) above the working platform (unless there is another adequate hand hold)
- Positioned so that vertical height of the ladder running between landing does not exceed 9 meters
- When moving or placing a ladder, be aware of overhead power lines and other electrical hazards

11.6 Placing Ladders

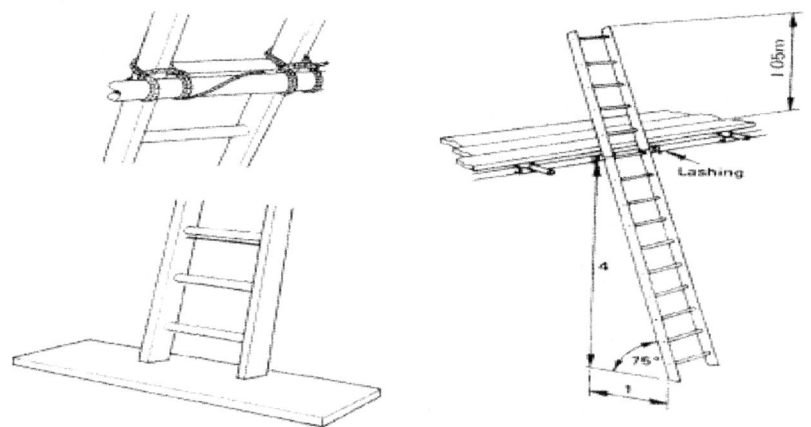

CHAPTER TWELVE

LADDER INSPECTION

- All ladders must be inspected prior to use.
- Things to look out for.
- Check to see if the ladder is damaged.
- Check the stills (sides) for cracks or splits.
- Check the rungs are all in place and the
- Supporting rods are under the rungs.

12.1 Access

- Working platforms must be provided, where necessary with access holes, which must not be more than 500mm wide, and as small as practicable in the other direction.

- Landing must be fitted with guard-rails and toe-boards, and no materials should be stored.

CHAPTER THIRTEEN

SYSTEM SCAFFOLDS

Common Types of System Scaffold
- Most systems are composed of standards with performed connectors welded at intervals along their length to which the ledgers are fitted with a proprietary clamping or wedging arrangement.

- Some earlier systems use tubes made into frames – typically H or X shapes, to avoid the need for bracing

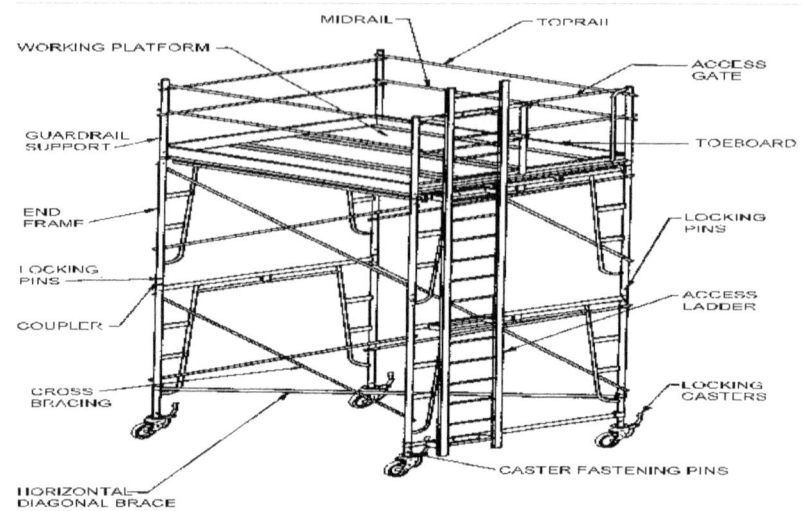

System Scaffolds

Ring Type   Cup lock System   Star System

CHAPTER FOURTEEN

HAZARDS IN CONSTRUCTION AND USE OF SCAFFOLD

Study has shown that about 72% of workers injured in scaffold accidents attributed the accident either to the planking or support giving way, or to the employee slipping or being struck by a falling object.

Scaffolds are integral to the construction industry with approximately 65% of the workforce involved in work from scaffolds. When used properly, scaffolds can save significant time and money.

Though they are convenient and necessary, there are four major hazards associated with worker injuries in relation to the construction and use of scaffold

4 Major Hazards: Scaffold Safety

14.1. Falls

Falls are attributed to the lack of guardrails, improper installation of guardrails and failure to use personal fall arrest systems when required. The OSHA standard requires fall protection must be used when work heights reach 10' or more. OSHA's standards represent the minimum level of protection; many general contractors require 100% fall protection at 6' or greater when working on scaffolds. These contractors are increasing safety margins by exceeding the minimum requirements of the OSHA standards.

Lack of proper access to the scaffold work platform is an additional reason for falls from scaffolds. Access in the form of a secured ladder, stair tower, ramp, etc. is required whenever there is 24" vertical change to an upper or lower level. The means of access must be determined before erection of the scaffold and employees are never allowed to climb on cross braces for either vertical or horizontal movement.

14.2. Scaffold collapse

The proper erection of a scaffold is essential in preventing this particular hazard. Before erecting the scaffold, a number of factors must be accounted for. The amount of weight the scaffold will be required to hold including the weight of the scaffold itself, materials, and workers must be considered. Foundation stability, placement of scaffold planks, distance from the scaffold to the work surface, and tie-in requirements are just a few of the other items that must be considered prior to constructing a scaffold.

A knowledgeable individual who can perform preplanning will reduce the chances of injury and save money for any task. However, when building, moving, or dismantling a scaffold, a knowledgeable person, also known as the scaffold competent person, must be present. A competent person must also inspect the scaffold daily to ensure the structure remains in a safe condition. Improper construction can lead to a total collapse of the scaffold or falling components – both of which can be fatal.

14.3. Struck by falling materials

Workers on scaffolds are not the only ones exposed to scaffold related hazards. Many individuals have been injured or killed due to being struck by materials or tools that have fallen from scaffold platforms. These people must be protected from falling objects. OSHA requires that this is done one of two ways. The first is to install toe boards or netting on work platforms to prevent these items from falling to the ground or lower level work areas. The other option is to erect barricades that physically prevent individuals from walking under work platforms.

Caution or Danger tape is often used in an attempt to keep people away from overhead hazards but is often disregarded or taken down creating possible struck by hazards. A more robust system such as plastic mesh or wooden barricades is generally more effective and much easier to maintain. When members of the public could potentially move close enough to be struck by falling objects, creating barriers to prevent them from entering the area where objects can fall is a recognized best practice. Regardless of the type of falling object protection used, it is crucial that other individuals on the work site are aware of the overhead work.

14.4. Electrocution

Once again we look to preplanning and the competent person to assure there are no electrical hazards present during scaffold use. A minimum of 10' must be maintained between the scaffold and electrical hazards. If this distance cannot be maintained, then the hazard must be de-energized or properly insulated by the power company. Coordination between the power company and the company erecting / using the scaffold cannot be over stated.

Lastly, all employees who work on scaffolds must have documented training. The training topics must include identification and prevention of fall hazards, falling tools and materials hazards, and knowledge of electrical hazards.

14.5 Summary on fall protection

- Fall protection is required when work heights reach 10 feet or more or according to your organizational standard.
- Provide proper access to the scaffold and never allow employees to climb on cross braces for horizontal or vertical movement.
- The scaffold competent person must be present when building, moving or dismantling the scaffold and must inspect it daily.
- Erect barricades to prevent individuals from walking under work platforms and place signs to warn those close by of the possible hazards.
- Maintain a minimum of 10 feet between the scaffold and any electrical hazard.
- Ensure all employees working on scaffolding have had proper training.
Scaffold safety starts from the ground up. Only safe work conditions and actions will prevent unnecessary injuries when working on these ever changing structures.
Editor's Note: This article was originally published in 2015, but has since been updated with more current information.

CHAPTER FIFTEEN

FALL PROTECTION WHILE BUILDING OR USING SCAFFOLD

Fall protection is the use of controls designed to protect personnel from falling or in the event they do fall, to stop them without causing severe injury. Typically, fall protection is implemented when working at height, but may be relevant when working near any edge, such as near a pit or hole, or performing work on a steep surface.

There are four generally accepted categories of fall protection: fall elimination, fall prevention, fall arrest and administrative controls. According to the US Department of Labour, falls account for 8% of all work-related trauma injuries leading to death.

In most work-at-height environments, multiple fall protection measures are used concurrently.

15.1 Fall elimination

Fall elimination is often the preferred way of providing fall protection. This entails finding ways of completing tasks without working at heights.

Hazard elimination is a hazard control strategy based on completely removing a material or process causing a hazard. Elimination is the most effective of the five members of the hierarchy of hazard controls in protecting workers, and where possible should be implemented before all other control methods. Many jurisdictions require that an employer eliminate hazards if it is possible, before considering other types of hazard control.

Elimination is most effective early in the design process, when it may be inexpensive and simple to implement. It is more difficult to implement for an existing process, when major changes in equipment and procedures may be required. Elimination can fail as a strategy if the hazardous process or material is reintroduced at a later stage in the design or production phases.

The complete elimination of hazards is a major component to the philosophy of Prevention through Design, which promotes the practice of eliminating hazards at the earliest design stages of a project. Complete elimination of a hazard is often the most difficult control to achieve, but addressing it at the start of a project allows designers and planners to make large changes much more easily without the need to retrofit or redo work.

15.2 Fall prevention

Fall prevention is a variety of actions to help reduce the number of accidental falls suffered by older people.

Falls and fall related injuries are among the most serious and common medical problems experienced by older adults. Nearly one-third of older persons fall each year, and half of them fall more than once. Over 3 million American over the age of 65 visited hospital emergency departments in 2015 due to fall related injuries with over 1.6 million being admitted. Because of underlying osteoporosis and decreased mobility and reflexes, falls often result in hip fractures and other fractures, head injuries, and even in older adults. Accidental injuries are the fifth most common cause of death in older adults. In around 75% of hip fracture patients, recovery is incomplete and overall health deteriorates.

The most consistently proven predictors of fall risk are history of a fall during the past year
and gait and balance abnormalities. Some studies (but not others) indicated that impaired vision,
certain medications (especially psychotropic drugs), decreased activities of daily living and impaired cognition are associated with a higher risk of falls. Furthermore, some interventions that have been shown to be effective in one country are not necessarily generalized to other populations. The contribution of orthostatic hypotension to fall risk remains uncertain.

- Fall guarding is the use of guard rails or other barricades to prevent a person from falling. These barricades are placed near an edge where a fall-hazard can occur, or to surround a weak surface (such as a skylight on a roof) which may break when stepped on.
- Fall restraint is a class of personal protective equipment to prevent persons who are in a fall hazard area from falling, e.g., fall restraint lanyards. Typically, fall restraint will physically prevent a worker from approaching an edges.

15.3 Fall arrest

Fall arrest is the form of fall protection that stops a person who has fallen.

Fall arrest is the form of fall protection which involves the safe stopping of a person already falling. It is one of several forms of fall protection, forms which also include fall guarding (general protection that prevents persons from entering a fall hazard area e.g., guard rails) and fall restraint (personal protection which prevents persons who are in a fall hazard area from falling, e.g., fall restraint lanyards).

15.4 Administrative controls

Administrative controls are used along with other measures, but they do not physically prevent a worker from going over an edge. Examples of administrative controls include placing a safety observer or warning line near an edge, or enforcing a safety policy which trains workers and requires them to adhere to other fall protection measures, or prohibiting any un-restrained worker from approaching an edge.

Administrative controls are training, procedure, policy, or shift designs that lessen the threat of a hazard to an individual.[1] Administrative controls typically change the behaviour of people (e.g., factory workers) rather than removing the actual hazard or providing personal protective equipment (PPE).

Administrative controls are fourth in larger hierarchy of hazard controls, which ranks the effectiveness and efficiency of hazard controls. Administrative controls are more effective than PPE because they involve some manner of prior planning and avoidance, whereas PPE only serves only as a final barrier between the hazard and worker. Administrative controls are second lowest because they require workers or employers to actively think or comply with regulations and do not offer permanent solutions to problems. Generally, administrative controls are cheaper to begin, but they may become more expensive over time as higher failure rates and the need for constant training or re-certification eclipse the initial investments of the three more desirable hazard controls in the hierarchy

CHAPTER SIXTEEN

SCAFFOLD INSPECTION

Scaffolds can collapse due to instability or overloading. Always inspect scaffoldings to make sure hazards do not result in tragedies.

16.1 When Should You Inspect Scaffolding?

As per OSHA regulations, 29 CFR 1926.451, scaffolding should be inspected:

- After installation / before first use.
- At least every week.
- Every time after adverse weather conditions like high wind which can affect a scaffold's structural integrity

16.2 Who Should Inspect the Scaffolding?

Scaffolding should be inspected by a competent person whose combination of knowledge, training and experience is appropriate for the type and complexity of the scaffold and who has the authorization to take prompt corrective measures to eliminate identified hazards around scaffolds.

16.3 How to Inspect Scaffolding Safety?

Employers should strive to protect their employees from common scaffold-related hazards such as falls, falling objects, structural instability, electrocution, and overloading. Here's is a checklist for periodic inspection of a scaffold. Inspection should be carried out for all the following components of a scaffold:

16.4 Scaffold Base and Structure

1. De-energize power lines near scaffolds and ensure there are no power lines, tools or materials within 10 feet of scaffoldings.

Keep scaffold away from electrical lines

2. Check if the type of scaffold is right for the loads, materials, workers and weather conditions.
3. Inspect footings to see if they are level, sound, firm, and can support the loaded scaffold.
4. Ensure that the legs, posts, frames and uprights are on baseplates and mudsills.
5. Ensure there are no bends, holes, cracks, rust, pits, welding splatter, broken or, and non-compatible parts in the metal components or scaffold.
6. Check for safe access. The cross-braces should not be used as ladder for access or exit.

7. A competent person must inspect ropes (in case of suspended scaffolds) for defects prior to each work shift and after every occurrence that could affect the rope's integrity.

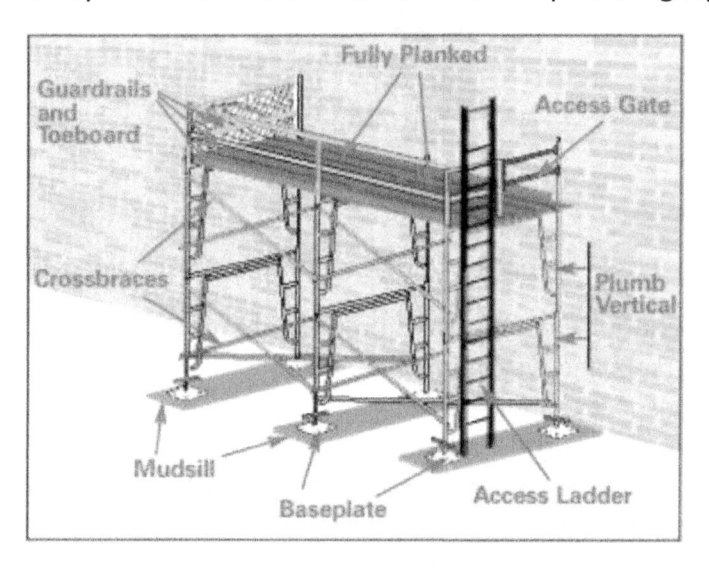

Here's an illustration showing different parts of a scaffolding that need to be inspected **[Source: OSHA]**

16.5 Planks

1. Inspect wooden planks and ensure there are no cracks or splits greater than 1/4-inch, long end splits, several large loose knots, warps greater than 1/4 inch, boards and ends with gouges, mold, separated laminate(s), and grain sloping

greater than 1 in 12 inches from the long edge. Planks must be scaffold grade lumber or equivalent.

Plank has a long split and unable to bear load

Plank with notches (small checks on the end)

2. Planks that deflect 1 /60 of the span or 2 inches in a 10-feet wooden plank, are damaged and should not be used.

Plank with checks (cracks that are only on the surface)

3. Ensure planks are close together, with spaces no greater than 1 inch around uprights.
4. 10-foot or shorter planks must be 6 to 12 inches over the centreline of the support. Longer planks should not be more than 18 inches over the end.

Platform

- Ensure that the platform is 14 inches or less from the wall or 18 inches or less away if plastering/stuccoing.
- Make sure there are guardrails and mid-rails on platforms where work is being done
- Check for workers under the platform and supplement protection from falling objects or barricade the area.
- Ensure that workers wear hard hats and fall protection.

NOTICE
HARD HATS AND FALL PROTECTION MUST BE WORN
WHEN WORKING ON SCAFFOLDING

5. Make sure braces, tie-ins and guying is used at each end, vertically and horizontally, and is done according to the scaffold manufacturer's instructions. This will prevent tipping.

CHAPTER SEVENTEEN

SCAFFOLD TAGGING AND INSPECTION

All scaffolds shall be inspected and marked with proper identification tags by a competent person. Untagged scaffold should not be used. Scaffold tag should be fastened to the access ladder or near the stairway at the eye level so it is easy to locate. The Scaffolding Inspector shall place a weather proof plasticised or equivalent colour coded label (SCAFFTAG) at each access point and at the boundary of each scaffold section from the initial erection stage until final dismantling.

It shall clearly state if the scaffold is "**READY FOR USE**" or "**NOT TO BE USED**". In addition the label shall state:

- Date erected, with name and initials of Scaffolding Foreman/ Supervisor.
- Maximum loading kN/m^2.
- Date inspected, with foreman name and Scaffolding Supervisor's signature.

Green Tags: When this scafftag is green it means that the scaffold is safe to use.

Identify scaffolds which have been modified to meet work requirements, and as a result could present a hazard to the user

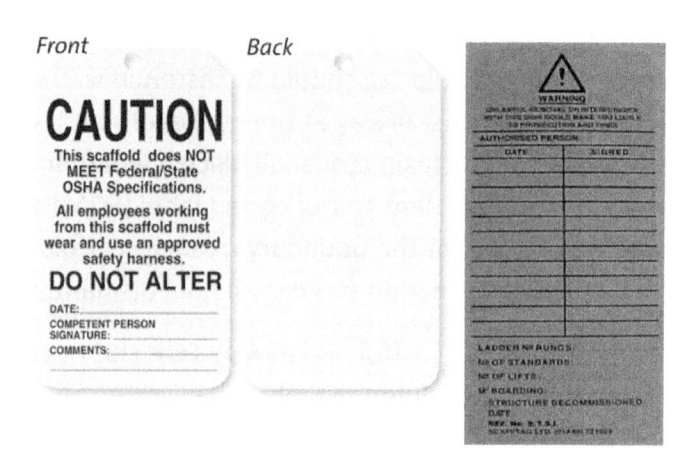

Front *Back*

CAUTION
This scaffold does NOT MEET Federal/State OSHA Specifications.
All employees working from this scaffold must wear and use an approved safety harness.
DO NOT ALTER
DATE:
COMPETENT PERSON SIGNATURE:
COMMENTS:

- Yellow "Caution" tag indicates special requirements for safe use. It allows the erecting crew to identify which portion of the scaffold is incomplete.
- Potential hazard and preventative measures are marked on the back of the tag. The information also contains the name of the client company representative authorizing the use of scaffold.
- Yellow tag should not to be removed until the scaffold is safe to use and inspected by a "competent person."
- Based on the results of that inspection, yellow tag should be replaced by appropriate tag (red or green).

Red Tags: This means that the scaffold platform is unsafe and must not be used by anybody except by certified scaffolder only for the purpose of rectifying or dismantling.

Front

DANGER

DO NOT USE THIS SCAFFOLD KEEP OFF

This scaffold is being erected, taken down or has been found defective.

DO NOT ALTER

DATE:
COMPETENT PERSON
SIGNATURE:
COMMENTS:

Back

SCAFFTAG

REF NO.

DO NOT USE SCAFFOLD

CHAPTER EIGHTEEN

SCAFFOLD CHECKLIST

Short checklist

Check at each inspection that your scaffold does not have these faults:

Footings — Yes No NA RM
Soft and uneven
No base plates
No sole boards
Undermined

Bracing — Yes No NA RM
Facade and ledger
Some missing
Loose
Wrong fittings

Ties — Yes No NA RM
Some missing
Loose

Standards
Not plumb
Jointed at same height
Wrong spacing
Damaged

Putlogs and transoms
Loose
Wrongly spaced
Wrongly supported

Boarding
Bad boards
Trap boards
Incomplete boarding
Insufficient supports

Ledgers
Loose
Not level
Joint in same bays
Damaged

Couplings
Wrong fitting
No check couplers
Loose
Damaged

Guard-rails and toe-boards
Loose
Wrong height
Some missing

Bridles
Weak support
Wrong spacing
Wrong couplings

Ladders
Not tied
Damaged
Insufficient length

SCAFFOLD INSPECTION CHECKLIST

Company Name:	Scaffold Location:			
Completed by:	Date:		Time:	
SAFETY CHECKS		Yes	No	Comments
Scaffold components, planking/decking in good condition? Planks graded for scaffold?				
All scaffold components in place and no defects?				
Competent person in charge of erection/inspection?				
Mud Sills properly placed and adequate sized when required?				
Screw jacks being used to level and plumb scaffold when required?				
Base plates and/or screw jacks in firm contact with mudsills and frame?				
Scaffold is level and plumb?				
Scaffold legs braced, with braces properly attached?				
Guard railing in place on all open sides and ends?				
Visual check to verify clamps secured in place?				
Scaffold secured to structure to prevent movement?				
Brackets, tube and clamp, and accessories properly placed with wedges tightened?				
Area around scaffold has been secured/roped off?				
Planks have minimum 12" overlap and extend 6" beyond supports?				
Toe boards properly installed when required?				
Proper access to get on and off the scaffold? Ladder secured in place?				
Scaffold control tag has been signed and approved for use?				
If inspection reveals scaffold is unsafe to use, has "Do Not Use" tag been placed at all access points?				
Signature:				

CHAPTER NINETEEN

INSPECTION REPORT

Report of inspection on scaffolding

The Construction (Health, Safety and Welfare) Regulations 1996, Regulation 30

Inspection carried out on behalf of...

Inspection carried out by..

Address of site...

Date and time of inspection	Description of place of work, or part inspected	Details of any matter identified giving rise to the health and safety of any person	Details of any action taken as a result of any matter identified	Details of any further action required

CHAPTER TWENTY

HANDING OVER CERTIFICATE

SCAFFOLDING - HANDING OVER CERTIFICATE

Contractor: .... Date: ....

Site: .... Time: ....

Description of section handed over: ....
....
....

Drawing No: ....
(where applicable)

Scaffolding as described above has now been completed and complies with the Construction (Health, Safety and Welfare) Regulations, 1996. It is structurally sound and should only be used and loaded in accordance with our Quotation No:

(....)

a) Use only for: ....

b) Loading to be: .... working lifts with distributed

   Load of: .... (kN/M2 lbs/ft2 per lift)

The detailed requirements of the Regulations with regard to guardrails - working platforms - toeboards - bracing and ties have been complied with.

In order to comply with Regulation 29 of the Construction (Health, Safety and Welfare) Regulations 1996, this scaffold must be inspected before being taken into use for the first time, at regular intervals not exceeding 7 days since the last inspection, after any event likely to have affected its strength or stability and after any substantial addition, dismantling or other alteration. In order to comply with Regulation 30, particulars of each inspection must be recorded in a Report of Inspection.

It is also the responsibility of every employer under Regulation 3 to see that the requirements of the Regulations which apply to his own men are complied with.

This Scaffold has / has not (delete as appropriate) been designed to take tarpaulin sheets (or other windsails).

Scaffold Contractor: ....

Depot: ....

Certificate received on behalf of the Contractor: ....

CHAPTER TWENTY ONE
COMMON MISTAKES MADE WITH SCAFFOLDING

There are so many small mistakes that can be made while using scaffolding that can lead to big accidents; here is 5 common ones:

21.1 **Workers who are not trained.** Like other professionals in the construction industry, knowing your job site and equipment is important to prevent problems and injuries. Those who are not trained for scaffolding often do not understand how fall protection works, their immediate surroundings, or common sounds of danger.

21.2 **Not building the scaffolding correctly.** Scaffolding can be a complex structure to erect, and if done incorrectly, can lead to collapse. We always suggest following OSHA standards and maintenance for scaffolding as to keep your equipment in the best shape, avoid fines, and keep your crew safe.

21.3 **Not using the correct fall protection.** When you have workers suspended on a tall landing like scaffolding, fall protection is essential to avoiding some major injuries. These extra steps keep your workers on the scaffolding, as well as their tools and materials. Investing in these details can help prevent future damages.

21.4 **Falling objects causing injury.** As a result of improper fall protection, it isn't uncommon falling debris, tools, or other objects have injured workers below. Netting, foot boards, and rails are great tools to combat these problems, and help avoid falling objects in the future.

21.5 **Ignoring or failing to note other external risks.** When scaffolding is constructed, it is almost daunting how tall it can be. With that height, it can often lead to risk regarding electrical work. Though injury in this regard is often less, the damage caused by high voltages can lead to fatal injury if not dealt with before work begins.

CHAPTER TWENTY TWO

COMMON FAULTS IN SCAFFOLD STRUCTURES

Scaffolds are used by builders and construction workers to elevate themselves, materials and equipment. Sadly, however, what goes up on scaffolding sometimes comes down suddenly and unexpectedly, leading to injuries or death. OSHA statistics indicate that scaffolding accidents result in 4,500 injuries and over 60 deaths each year and that almost 30 percent of all workplace deaths from falls involve scaffolding or ladders.

According to a recent OSHA report, more than 70 percent of scaffold accident injuries are caused by:

- Scaffold support or planking giving way, either due to defective or damaged equipment or improper assembly, leading to falls and injuries to those below
- Slipping or tripping while on a scaffold due to such factors as slippery surfaces, an unsafe incline or insufficient planking, leading to falls where guardrails, a safety harness, or proper training were lacking.
- Falling objects hitting either a worker on a scaffold or those below.

Other scaffold accidents can involve improper placement of scaffolds and equipment too close to power or other utility lines, leading to electrocution.

The pictures below show common faults in scaffold structures:

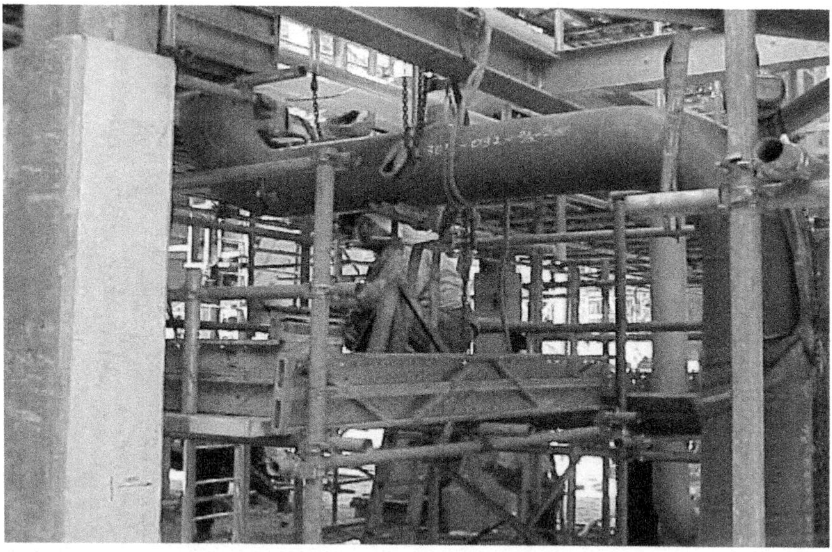

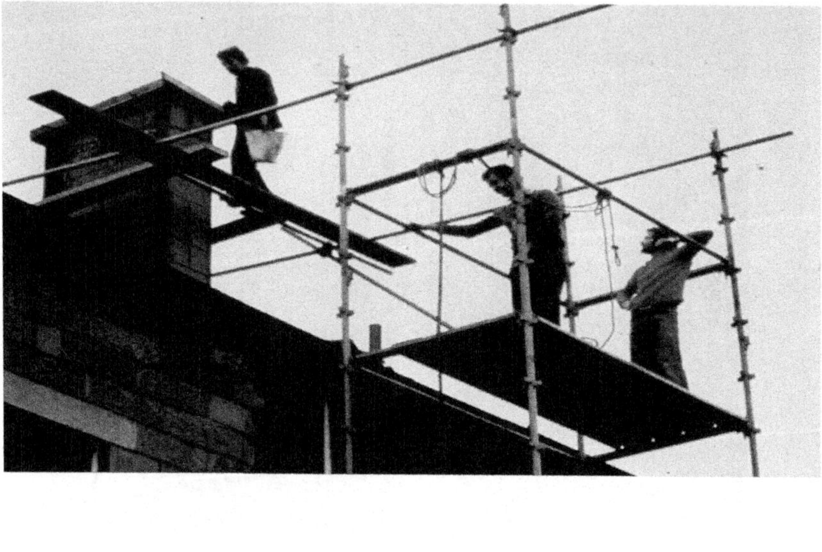

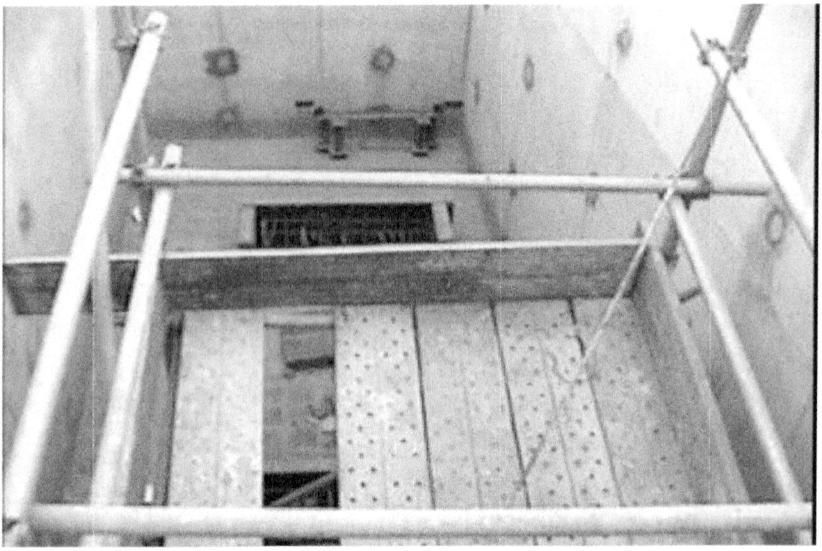

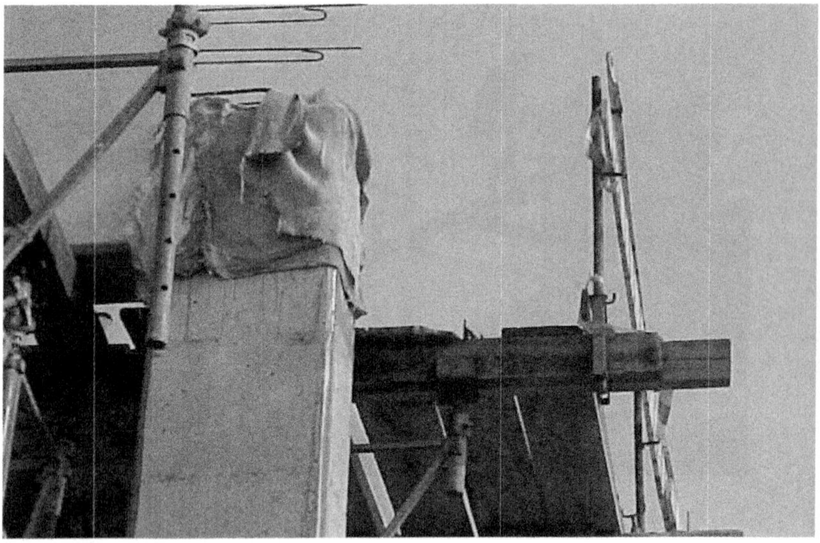

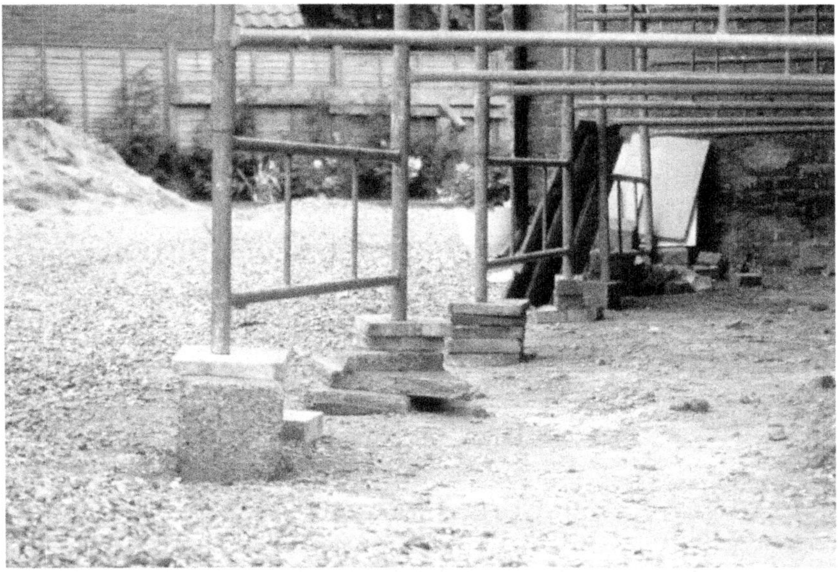

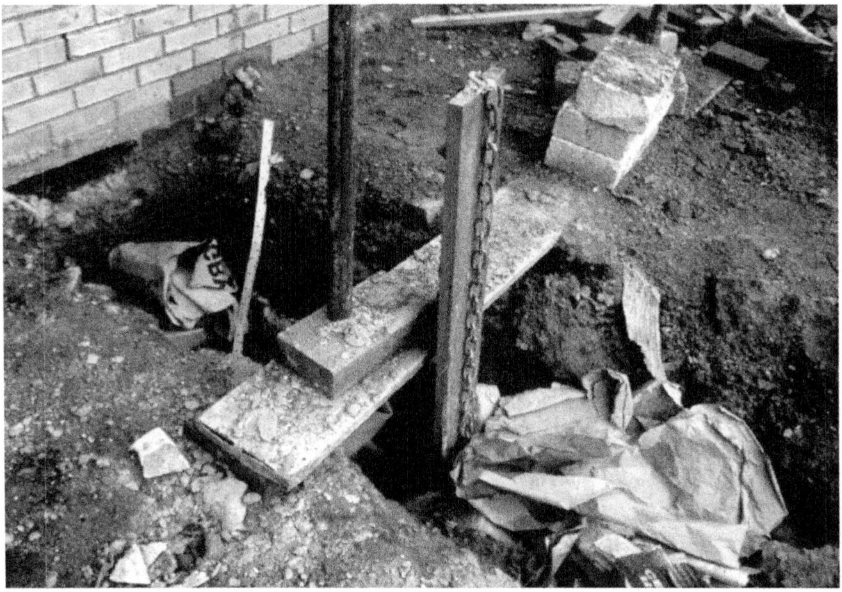

TWENTY THREE

CONCLUSION

Remember to:

- Use appropriate scaffold construction methods
    - Erect, move, or alter scaffold properly
    - Protect from falling objects or tools
    - Ensure stable access
- Use a competent person
    - Train on scaffold construction and the hazards involved with scaffolds
    - Inspect scaffold before each shift and after alterations
    - Determine fall protection requirements

The fall won't hurt, but the sudden stop will!

✓ **Look after yourself**

✓ **Look after the people around you.**

REFERENCES

1. en.wikipedia.org
2. oshatraining.org
3. nationwideladder.com
4. sommerspe.com
5. Oil and Gas exploration and production document
6. SCiN scaffold manual

Printed in Great Britain
by Amazon